HEARTBREAKS
AND
Rainbows

LATOYA BROWN

Published 2024

Printed in the United States of America

First Edition

ISBN (softcover): 978-1-963380-41-5
ISBN (e-book): 978-1-963380-42-2

For information, address:

Holzer Books LLC
8 The Green, Ste. A
Dover, Delaware 19901 USA

For information about special discounts available for bulk purchases, sales promotions, and educational needs, contact:

info@holzerbooksllc.com
+1 (888) 901-7776

Contents

A Deeper Understanding

I never understood what it was like being on the other side

To the pain and the hurt, I've been blind

Now I've seen it, my eyes are open wide

To the long days and nights you spent by my side

To all your hopes and prayers that kept me alive

When I needed you, you were always there

When I couldn't move a muscle, you dressed me, combed my hair

Never once did you give up on me, nor did you complain

You stayed with me during sunshine and rain

I hope you never learn what it's like to bury a child

Because I know that would tear you up inside

I'll never completely understand the pain and suffering you went through

But just in case you've never heard me say it... "Thank You"

Heartbreak

I'm up early on a beautiful island, and all I can think about is you

How you're doing me wrong, and you don't even have the guts to tell me we're through

What's going on? Is it your wife? Are you not interested anymore, or are you just busy?

I know... you saw some other chick that you like. So, who is she?

Is she pretty? Is she smart? Does she have a bigger heart than me?

Is she nice? More compatible? Does she have congeniality?

The other day you called me and told me that I was yours

You wooed me into thinking that we had so much more

More than a friendship, if you can even call it that

Right now, the only thing I feel like is your doormat

You walk all over me, leaving behind your dirt

Then you say goodbye, leaving me nothing but hurt

You don't call me for a week...sometimes two

Then you expect me to be okay and smile for you

But how can I smile when all I get from you is hurt and pain

And everything I do, or have done, for you is in vain

You're going to make me like somebody else

If you don't watch yourself

So, stop pushing me away if you want me to stick around

Because one day you might look around and I'll be nowhere to be found

I Want To Fall In Love

I want to fall in love
But my time has yet to come
I'm trying to be patient
But I think I might just succumb...
To the next man who looks my way
The next man who pays me a compliment
The next man who shows interest
I'm ready to be fully compliant
I'm ready for walks in the park
I'm ready for late night talks
I'm ready for flowers and dinners
If only I could find myself a winner
I'm ready for marriage and buying a house
I'm ready for babysitters and late nights out
I'm ready for family vacations and family pics
I'm ready for nights on the couch with Netflix
Where is this man who can fulfill my dreams?
Where is the one who will be my Supreme?
I'm hoping that he will soon appear
I'm ready to be called "My Dear"

I'm So Hot

♥

I'm so hot. Let me tell you what I got

I've got lips for days

I've got tits that stay

Perky and round

No sagging down

I'm so hot. Let me tell you what I've got

I've got long, skinny stems

I've got skin glistening like gems

Shiny, smooth, the color of chocolate

Men get excited just caressing it

I'm so hot. Let me tell you what I've got

I've got creamy little thighs

I've got almond-shaped eyes

Brown and deep

My soul's secrets, they keep

I'm so hot. Let me tell you what I've got

I've got a round little ass

I've got small, soft hands

With long, skinny fingers

And a touch that lingers

I'm so hot. Let me tell you what I've got

I've got a big, beautiful smile that you can see from a mile

I'm Sorry

I'm sorry you were told you were born to lose
I'm sorry that you keep being misused
I'm sorry that you're being played by your girl
I'm sorry you don't know that you could own the world
I'm sorry you don't know that you have so much potential
I'm sorry you don't know that you could be positively influential
I'm sorry you don't know how deep your eyes are—those baby blues
I'm sorry you don't know how much I admire you
I'm sorry you don't know that you have great lips
I'm sorry you don't know that you have a breathtaking kiss
I'm sorry that I didn't meet you three months ago
Maybe then it would have been a different show
But I guess that is just the way that life goes
Saying "I'm sorry" does not take back all of your pain
Saying "I'm sorry" is not going to stop the rain
It is not going to make you see that you have a beautiful soul
Nor will it help you to accomplish all of your hidden goals
I just want you to realize that in the end
To change your life, you need to realize who are your real friends

If Only

If only you could see me the way they do
If only you could see that you are special too
If only you weren't so intimidated
If only when I came around you I didn't feel so sedated
If only you knew that everything you need is here in me
If only I could pull that blindfold off and make you see
If only we were in a different time, a different place
If only nine months ago you had used up that space
If only I could see ahead, into the future
If only I could snap my finger and make you more mature
If only you could see into my heart
If only we could have a brand-new start
If only she hadn't shown up at the shop
If only you had known that you shouldn't have stopped...
...stopped the good thing that we had going on
...stopped knowing your right from your wrong
...stopped the fun that we were having
...stopped all of our playing and laughing
If only you had not stopped our fun to be hurt by someone who claimed she was still in
love
If only you could see that I'm your savior...sent from above

Insight

You seem to think that I've lost my trust in you
But the only thing that I've lost is my patience
You don't know that I'm intimidated by you too
So you keep me at arm's length, guessing...waiting
You're not used to girls like me, I can tell
You're not used to good girls who treat you well
You're used to girls who sleep around
Who put their business out all over town
Never have you had a girl with such class and intelligence,
A girl who can challenge you mentally
A girl with such innocence
A girl who excites you physically
A girl who knows what's in your soul
A girl who can empathize with you
A girl who can help you realize AND conquer your goals
A girl who actually paid attention in school
For reasons unknown, I believe everything you tell me
And it's not just because, in the beginning, you said you would help me
It's not because you take me out and open doors
It's because inside of you I see so much more...
I see kindness, I see warmth
I see wisdom, I see intelligence

I see induration, I see wear and tear
I see destitution, I see vigilance
I see determination, I see fear
I see passion, I see affection
I see a better man by next year

Late

The rent check is due
But the landlord can't find you
You're accruing late fees
While I'm praying on my knees
Praying this check doesn't bounce
Praying I don't get evicted from my house
I hear footsteps approaching the third floor
Boom, Boom, Boom... the knock on my door
The lady wants to know, "Where is the rent check?"
Why do I always get stuck with your mess?
So I call you, but there is no answer...
You're such a fucking bastard!

Night

Cars passing
Blinkers flashing
Sounds of a train
Smell of a coming rain
Planes flying by
In a star-filled sky
A spider building a web
My child asleep in her bed
Crickets chirping
Creatures lurking
A cool, gentle breeze
Sweeps through the fragile, wilting leaves
It gently stirs the water in the murky pond
The undulations move to the edges, but can't go beyond
Crisp, cool, calm, and clear
Affluent, ambient, and arctic, the air
I take a look around and inhale deeply
It's time to go in now...I'm feeling sleepy

Not Afraid To Die

Today I realized that I'm not afraid to die. If the Lord should take me now, I would be ready and willing to go to the place in the sky, where I don't have to worry about people hurting or killing each other.

Today I realized that I'm not afraid to die. I am looking forward to my time to go. Death is the one area of my life where I don't feel shy. It's also the one thing in my life that I know is certain...death.

Rainbow

I see a rainbow, big and bright
Giving off extraordinary rays of light
Red, yellow, purple, blue
Aqua green and orange too
A symbol of good fortune and hope
Tapering off at the mountain's slope
Clouds surround and attempt to cover
But none can conquer, and still it hovers

Reality

Everyday I'm in constant pain
My body and my joints ache
There's no relief in sight
Because there's nothing I can take
My heart does not beat the way that it should
My legs don't move the way they could
My joints snap, crackle, and pop
I wish there was something I could do to make them stop
Hospital bills come in the mail every day
I keep on paying, but they never go away
At 22 years old, I feel like I'm 75
Some days I wake up and I don't want to be alive
I get upset that He's kept my heart beating
I get upset that He didn't just take me while I was sleeping
I know that we all have our good days and our bad
I know that at some point everyone gets sad
But why does it seem like I have more bad days than good
Why does it seem that my life isn't going the way it should
I sometimes feel like running away
I wish that I had a secret hideaway
Do like they do in the movies and just skip town
But I guess I just have to face reality, as long as He's willing to keep me around

They Say

♥

They say God never gives us more than we can handle
But I'm starting to wonder if that's really true
They say we should live each moment like the last
And start each day anew
But how do you live each day like the last
When you're being haunted by a wicked past
And you're headed nowhere...fast?
They say you should stand strong and face whatever comes your way
But sometimes that seems impossible
They say the soul can't see a rainbow if the eyes never see a tear
My tears are unstoppable
So how come I've never seen a rainbow?
They say life is full of choices
But no one ever mentions all the fear
They say love is a wonderful thing
But no one ever mentions all the tears
All the times you cry in the middle of the night
After an argument or a horrible fight
Trying to keep the relationship together, with all of your might
They say you should never be afraid to die
Because when it's your time to go there is nothing you can do
But we should never be afraid to fight for our life

Because if it's not your time, you will know

Nothing in this world is ever for sure

But when you have something good, you need to hold on and don't let go

Who the hell is "they",

And what do they know anyway?

"They" probably have never been through any of this

So far as I'm concerned,

What "they" say is Bullshit!

Unanswered

What is the name of the gang that you're in? At what age did you start? Are you serious
about retiring?

Do you really think you have the heart?

How is that child that you told me about?

Do you sometimes wish that child was yours?

Will you only come to me when you're down and out?

Or are you looking for much more?

If you had to do it all again, would you still have gotten married?

Or would you have walked away?

Do you wish she had miscarried?

I wonder what you're like in bed. Are you gentle, or are you wild?

Do you have what it takes to make me scream really loud?

Afterwards, will you hold me and caress me just like a child?

When do I get to take a ride on your boat?

Or on the back of your motorcycle, the wind in my hair?

Is your home country beautiful?

One day, will you take me there?

Does your sister like me?

Does she think I'm pretty?

Do your friends like me too?

Do they find me witty?

So many questions that are going through my head

So many things that have been left unsaid

So many thoughts take over my brain and spread just like a cancer

But until I have the nerve to ask you, I guess they will all remain unanswered

Unsure

♥

You called me up because you wanted to talk
You said the upcoming week would bring a brand new start
But the only thing I've seen is unfulfilled plans
From someone who claims he wants to be a different man
How do you expect to change when you're stuck in the past?
On a sour relationship that just can't seem to last
Maybe you break plans because you need some time to yourself
Maybe you finally realize that solitude could help...
Help you clear your mind and start to move on
Help you see that your days of confusion and hurt could be gone
Whatever the reason is, you need to let me know
So I can either sit and be patient or turn around and go
If you want, I can be just a friend to you
But don't keep leading me on the way that you do
I need to know...are we through?

www.ingramcontent.com/pod-product-compliance
Lightning Source LLC
Chambersburg PA
CBHW031242120626
46545CB00003B/1246